CHILDREN'S PIANO PIECES THE WHOLE WORLD PLAYS

A COLLECTION OF MORE THAN ONE HUNDRED AND FIFTY TUNEFUL PIANO PIECES FOR JUVENILE PLAYERS, INCLUDING STANDARD TEACHING AND RECREATION PIECES, AND IN ADDITION A CON- SIDERABLE NUMBER OF NEW COMPOSITIONS

Grades I - II - III

Compiled and Edited

by

ALBERT E. WIER

Embassy Music Corporation
New York / London / Sydney / Cologne

7-95

International Standard Book Number: 0.8256.1002.8

Exclusive Distributors:
Music Sales Corporation
225 Park Avenue South, New York, NY 10003 USA
Music Sales Limited
8/9 Frith Street, London W1V 5TZ England
Music Sales Pty. Limited
120 Rothschild Street, Rosebery, Sydney, NSW 2018, Australia

Printed in the United States of America by
Vicks Lithograph and Printing Corporation

To the Music Lover

"CHILDREN'S PIANO PIECES" has a two-fold purpose—to serve equally well as a collection for teaching or for recreation. The pieces contained in it cover the first three grades of technical difficulty, (a graded index will be found in the back of the volume) and in the selection of each the elements of melody and rhythm have had primary consideration. The selection of compositions is of the most comprehensive character, ranging from little classics to folk-songs and dances of our own and other countries. In addition, those in search of new material will find an interesting group of tiny pieces by contemporary Russian composers which are without peer in their charming originality. In preparing this volume, the editor has carried uppermost in his mind that children must have much of light and little of shadow.

THE EDITOR

Alphabetical Index

Classified Index on Page 6 — Graded Index on Page 254.

Classified Index

CLASSICAL PIECES

MODERN PIECES

Alphabetical Index on Page 4 — Graded Index on Page 254.

MODERN PIECES (Continued)

LITTLE PIECES FROM THE OPERAS

FOLK-SONGS AND DANCES

Serenade

G. BACHMANN

Quick March

F. X. CHWATAL

In May

Grade I

FRANZ BEHR

Allegretto

Grade I

March From "Norma"

V. BELLINI.

Tempo di Marcia

Grade I

Little Playmates

F. X. CHWATAL.

The Fair

Grade I

C. GURLITT

Tick! Tack!

Grade I

FR. HUNTEN

At The Theatre

Grade I

Allegretto

FR. HUNTEN

Grade I

Waltz

FRANZ BEHR

The Little Ferryman

Grade I

GUSTAV LANGE

Allegretto non troppo

Star Song

CARL CZERNY.

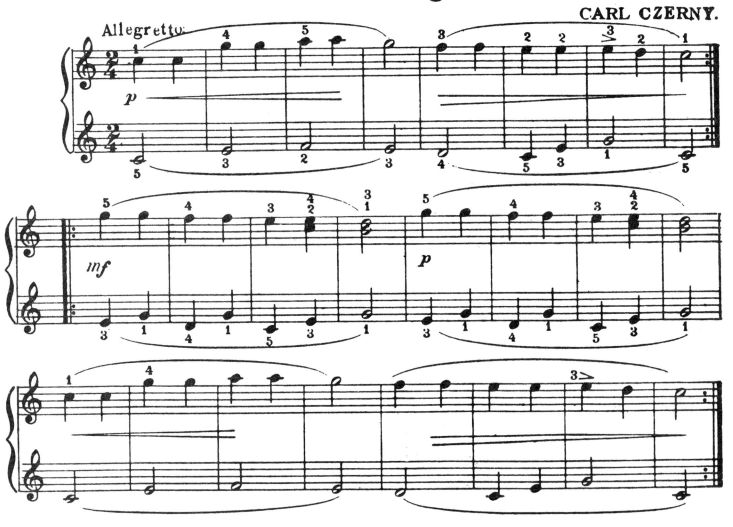

Grade I

When The Rain Stops

J. SCHMITT.

Grade I

Little Song

CARL CZERNY

Allegro

Restless Galop

Grade I

L. STREABBOG

Round And Round We Go

A. DIABELLI.

Short Song

C. GURLITT.

At The Fountain

Grade I

TH. OESTEN

Grade I

Petit Carnaval

WALTZ

L. STREABBOG.

D.S.al Fine

Grade I

The Bee-Hive

F.X.CHWATAL.

Rustic Dance

Grade II

FR. HUNTEN

Allegretto

Melody

R. SCHUMANN

Grade I

A Glorious Race

F. X. CHWATAL

Allegretto

The Wild Rose

Grade II

FR. SCHUBERT

Andantino con grazia

The First Violet

Grade II

FR. BEHR

Minuet

Grade II

J. S. BACH

Turkish March

Grade II

L. VAN BEETHOVEN

A Song Of Love

Grade II

S. JADASSOHN

Dialogue

C. REINECKE

Grade II

Andante tranquillo

Petite Valse

Grade II

H. REINHOLD

Leggiero e grazioso

Tranquility

Grade II

Fr. SPINDLER

Song Without Words

Grade II

XAVER SCHARWENKA

Andante con moto
espressivo

Grade II

Little Chatterbox

C. REINECKE

Allegro vivace assai

Melody

Grade II

Fr. THOME

Moderato

Parting Song

Grade II

C. REINECKE

The Angel Of Peace

Grade II

E. BRUNNER

Andante espressivo

Sonatina Movement

Grade II

M. CLEMENTI

Allegro con spirito

Fairy - Tale

TH. KULLAK

Grade II

Allegretto

Andante "Surprise" Symphony

Grade II

JOS. HAYDN

Funeral March

Grade II

FR. CHOPIN

Slumber Song

Grade II

Moderato

C. GURLITT

Robin Adair

The Happy Farmer

Grade II

R. SCHUMANN

Allegro animato

Huntsmen's Chorus

Grade II

C. M. Von WEBER

Heather Rose

G. LANGE

Andante cantabile

Content

Grade II

WILLY HERRMANN

Moderato

Italian Song

Grade II

P. TSCHAIKOWSKY

Song Of The Mermaids

(Oberon)

Grade II

C. M. Von WEBER

Andantino cantabile

Rataplan
(Daughter of the Regiment)

Grade II

G. DONIZETTI

Allegro con spirito

The Clock

Grade II

TH. KULLAK

Allegro vivace

The Skaters

Grade II

FR. BEHR

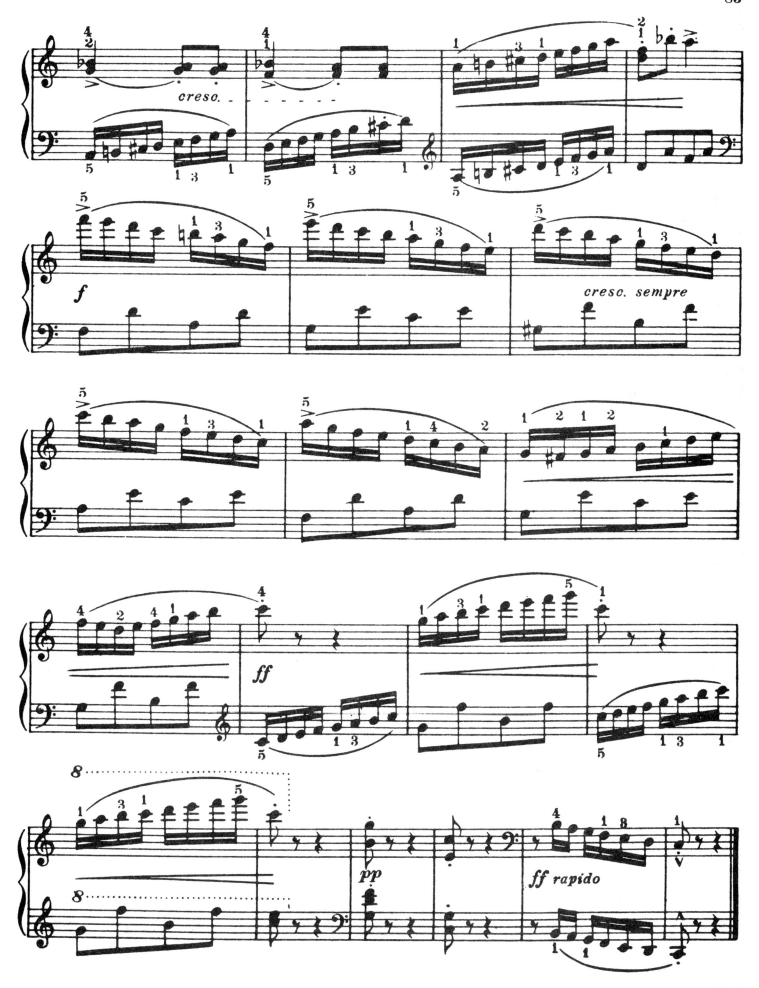

A Merry Frolic

Grade II

H. BERENS

Allegretto

Romance
(Fra Diavolo)

Grade II

Allegretto moderato

D. AUBER

Woodland Revery

Grade II

F. BEAUMONT

Gavotte

Grade II

J. S. BACH

Allegro moderato

Little Soldier's March

Grade II

L. KÖHLER

Moderato

Always Jolly

Grade II

C. KNAYER

Parade March

H. LICHNER

Grade II

D.C. al Fine

C.P.P.

Jolly Huntsman

G. MERKEL

Grade II

Allegro

Grade II

Russian Dance

Moderato

Child's Dreamland

Grade II

O. ROEDER

Ah! So Fair
(Martha)

Grade II

FR. von FLOTOW

Duke's Song
(Rigoletto)

Grade II

G. VERDI

A Winter's Tale

Grade II

A. CZIBULKA

Andante cantabile

Pearly Scales

Fr. SPINDLER

Grade II

Petite Piece

Grade II

A. GOEDICKE

Morning Prayer

Grade II

L. STREABBOG

Andante

ben marcato il canto

The Last Rose Of Summer
(Martha)

Grade II

FR. FLOTOW

Larghetto

Believe Me If All Those Endearing Young Charms

Grade II

Allegretto moderato

Irish Folk Song

Circle Dance

Grade II

N. von WILM

Vainly Asking

Grade II

H. E. BUTTON

Ave Maria

Grade II

C. REINECKE

Fun In The Country

Grade II

TH. OESTEN

In Rank And File

Grade II

G. LANGE

Joyfulness

Grade II

Moderato

Fr. SPINDLER

O Thou Joyful Day

Grade II
Andante

Air
(Lucia)

Grade II

G. DONIZETTI

The Harmonious Blacksmith

Grade II

G. F. HÄNDEL

Andante grazioso

Minuet
(Don Juan)

W. A. MOZART

Grade II

Moderato

C. P. P.

Duet
(Faust)

Grade II

CH. GOUNOD

Andante

Silhouette

Grade II

A. REINHOLD

Waltz
(Faust)

Grade II

CH. GOUNOD

Tempo di Valse

The Merry Mandarin

Grade II

ED. POLDINI

Vivace

Rondo

Grade II

J. L. DUSSEK

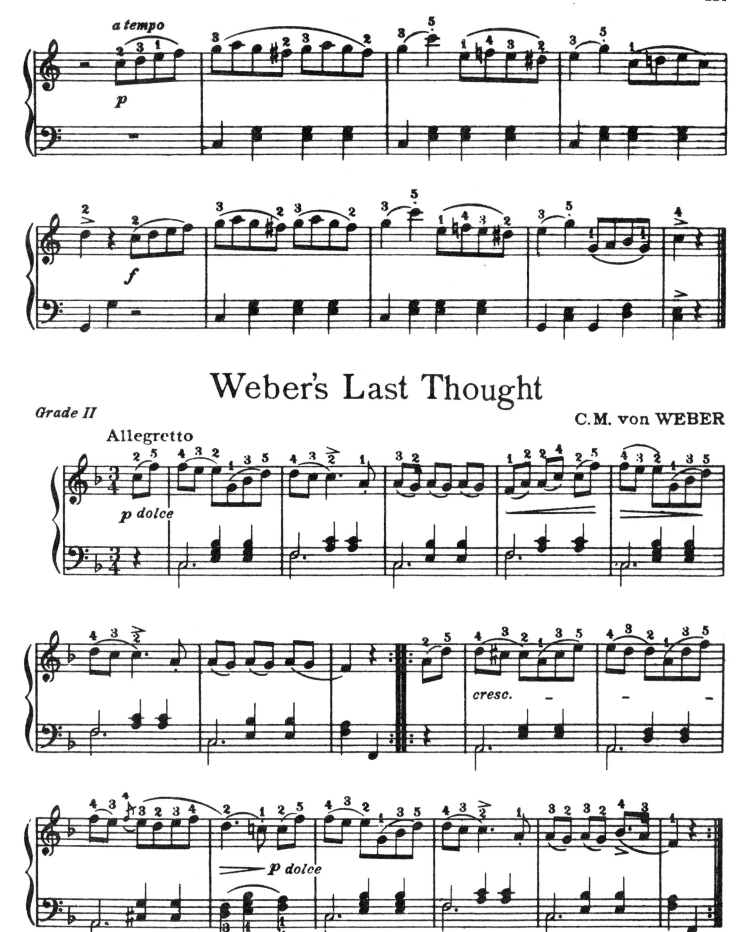

Weber's Last Thought

Grade II

C.M. von WEBER

Sunny Morning

Grade II

C. GURLITT

The Blue Bells Of Scotland

Grade II

Scotch Folk Song

Andantino

The Wayside Rose

Grade II

OTTO FISCHER

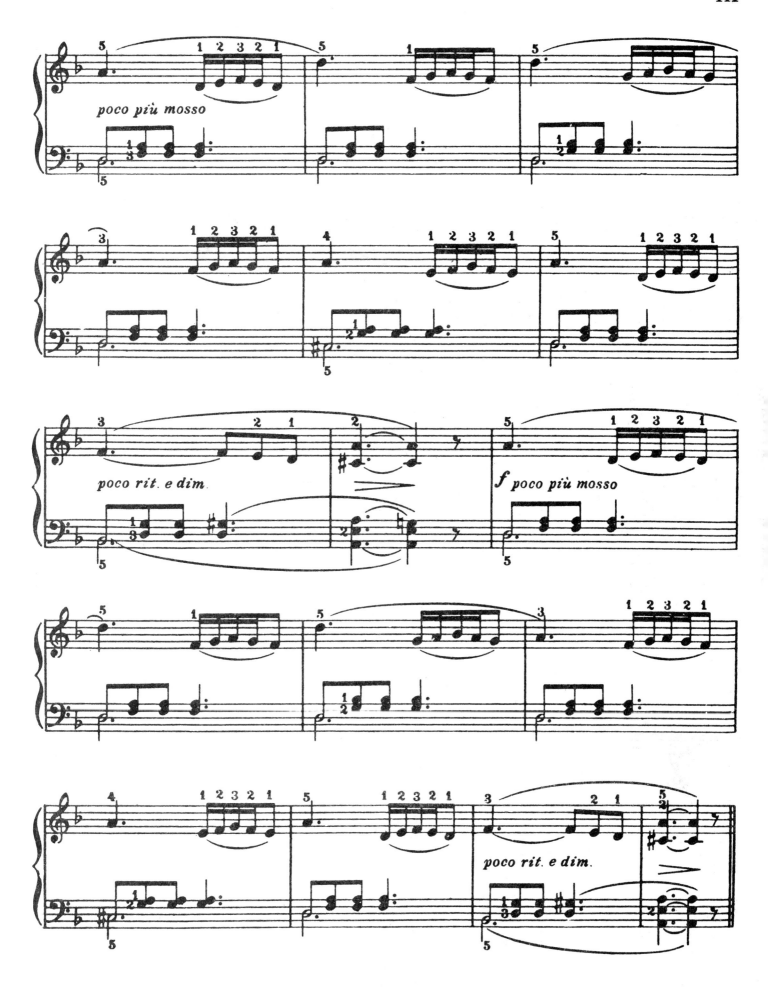

Tempo I

Soldiers' March

R. SCHUMANN

Grade II

Allegro deciso

Merry

Grade II

PAUL ZILCHER

Allegro

Gavotte

Grade III

J. S. BACH

Cradle Song

Grade II

C. M. von WEBER

Album Leaf

Grade III

ED. GRIEG

Allegretto

Hunting Song

Grade III

R. SCHUMANN

The Old Oaken Bucket

Grade III

Nocturne

Grade III

H. LICHNER

Prelude

Grade III

FR. CHOPIN, Op. 28, № 20

The Christmas Tree
Entrance March

Grade III

N. W. GADE

Little Mischief

Grade III

ED. POLDINI

Gavotte

Grade III

Moderato

J. S. BACH

Melody

Grade III

CH. KNAYER

Andante espressivo

mf

legato

dolce

cresc.

doloroso agitato

f

rallentando

The Red, White And Blue

Grade III

Old Black Joe

Grade III

STEPHEN FOSTER

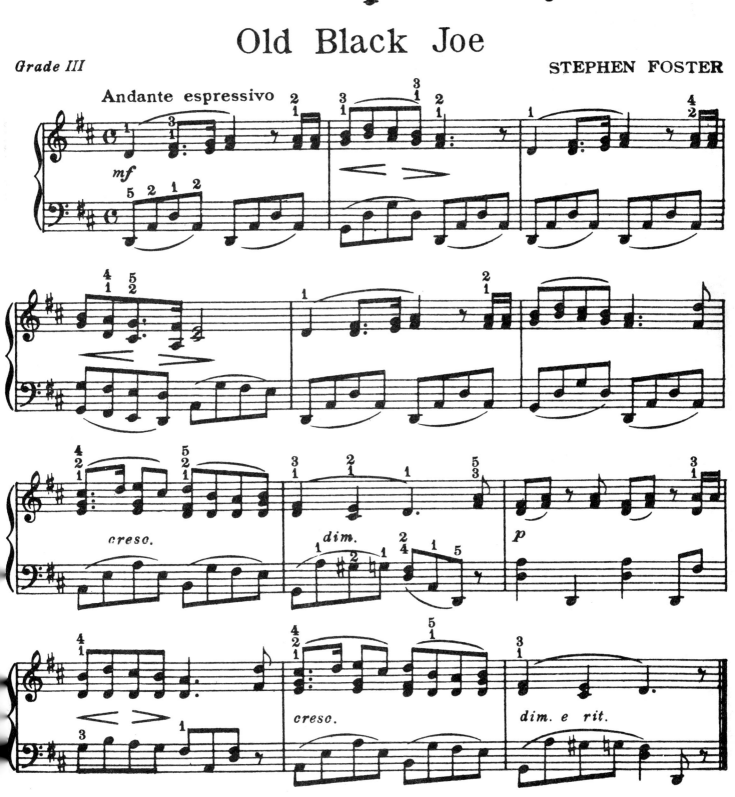

Melody in F
(Juvenile Edition)

Grade III

A. RUBINSTEIN

Auld Lang Syne

Grade III

Moderato

General Bum Bum

Grade III

ED POLDINI

Angel Voices

Grade III

E. BATISTE

Andante

Dreaming

Grade III

PAUL ZILCHER

Home, Sweet Home

Grade III

HENRY R. BISHOP

Annie Laurie

Grade III

Scotch Folk Song

Holiday-Time

Grade III

A. GOEDICKE

Giocoso.

Barcarolle
(Tales of Hoffmann)

Grade III

J. OFFENBACH

Sextette
(Lucia)

Grade III

G. DONIZETTI

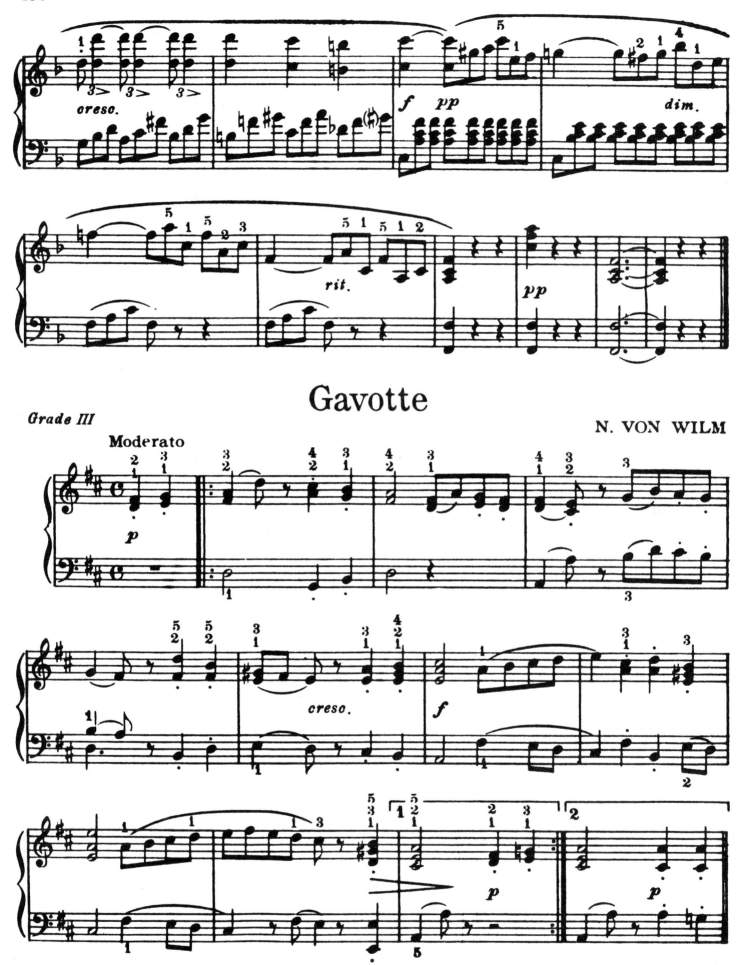

Gavotte

Grade III

N. VON WILM

Moderato

Home To Our Mountains
(Il Trovatore)

Grade III

G. VERDI

Andantino

Serenade

Grade III

CH. GOUNOD

Shepherd's Idyl

Grade III

CARL HEINS

Moderato con moto

The Star Spangled Banner

Grade III

Larghetto

Grade III

W. A. MOZART

Larghetto cantabile

Andante

XAVIER SCHARWENKA

Grade III

The Old Folks At Home

STEPHEN FOSTER

Grade III

Who Is Sylvia?

Grade III

FR. SCHUBERT

Good Night

Grade III

A. LOESCHHORN

Allegretto tranquillo

Andante

L. van BEETHOVE

Grade III

Andante
(Rinaldo)

Grade III

G. F. HÄNDEL

Last Night

Grade III

H. KJERULF

Spring Song

Grade III

F. MENDELSSOHN

Allegro grazioso

Evening Prayer

Grade III

C. REINECKE

The Lawn Party

Grade III

K. EIGES

Song Of The Morning

Grade III

W. LANDSTEIN

Coronation March
(The Prophet)

Grade III

G. MEYERBEER

Tempo di Marcia, molto maestoso

Contemplation

Grade III

H. LICHNER

Folk Song

Grade III

F. MENDELSSOHN

Andantino

Valse Lente

X. SCHARWENKA

Grade III

Prelude

Grade III

FR. CHOPIN, Op. 28, Nº 7

Mazurka

Grade III

FR. CHOPIN

Fairy Tale

Grade III

H. REINHOLD

Andante con moto

Fragrant Violet

Grade III

F. SPINDLER

Andante Cantabile

The Marseillaise

Grade III

French National Song

America

Grade III

Andante

C. P. P.

Petite Valse

Grade III

P. TSCHAIKOWSKY

Gazing At The Stars

Grade III

A. DIABELLI

Andante cantabile

The Music Box

Grade III

ED. POLDINI

Allegretto vivace

Night Song

Grade III

FR. BEHR

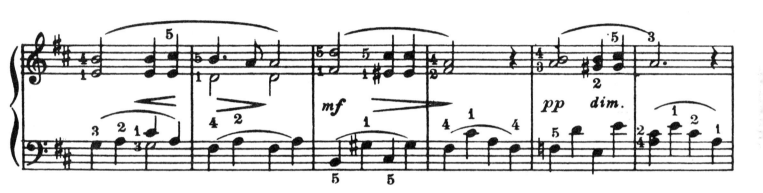

Moment Musical

Grade III

FR. SCHUBERT

Morning Greeting

Grade III

FR. SCHUBERT

Moderato

Scherzetto

V. SELIVANOV

Vivo leggiero

Hungarian Dance

Grade III

R. KLEINMICHEL

Andante
(Orpheus)

Grade III

C. W. GLUCK

Mayday March

Grade III

FRANZ BEHR

D.C. al Fine

Happy Moments

Grade III

N. LADOUKHIN

Minuet

Grade III

L. van BEETHOVEN

Moderato

Graded Index

GRADE I

GRADE II

Alphabetical Index on Page 4 — Classified Index on Page 6.

GRADE II (Continued)

GRADE III